Julia Roberts. What do people know about her?

She's smart and beautiful. She's a famous actress, and people love her movies. She's a superstar! And, people always remember her smile. This big smile brings light into a room. Suddenly, people are happy.

But what is the story behind this smile? How does a little girl from a quiet town find the big lights of Hollywood?

Julia Fiona Roberts is born in Atlanta on October 28, 1967. Her brother, Eric, is born in 1956, and her sister, Lisa, arrives in 1965. The three children live in a house with much love. But there are problems, too. Julia's father and mother, Walter and Betty, love the theater. They start a school for young actors in a big house in Atlanta. They work all day and night, but there's never much money.

In 1972, Walter and Betty get a divorce. Lisa and Julia live with their mother in Smyrna, Georgia. Eric lives with his father in Atlanta. Lisa and Julia don't often see Eric and their father. But Walter loves them and writes many letters to them. Then, in 1977, he suddenly dies.

At twelve years old Julia has her beautiful smile. But behind the smile she is not always happy.

From 1982 to 1985, Julia is happy at Campbell High School. She likes games, dances, music, movies, and people. She has many friends—but not many boyfriends—and she has fun. She's a good student, too. Julia finishes school and moves to New York. Eric and Lisa live there, too. Eric's an actor. Maybe Julia can be an actress.

Julia has a good time in New York. She goes places with Eric. She meets some important people. She doesn't go to actors' school, but she looks for roles in TV and in movies. In 1986, Eric has a role in a new movie, *Blood Red*. The director is looking for an actress for a small role.

Eric says, "My sister can be my sister in this movie."

Blood Red is the first movie with Julia Roberts.

In 1987, Julia gets work in two movies. She's good in
Satisfaction and she meets her first important boyfriend,
the actor, Liam Neeson. He's in *Satisfaction*, too. They
fall in love and move to California.

Then Julia gets the big role of Daisy in *Mystic Pizza*. She
has fun with the actors, and many people like the movie.
Now Hollywood directors know the name Julia Roberts.

In 1988, director Herb Ross wants Meg Ryan for *Steel Magnolias*, but she's making *When Harry Met Sally*. Sally Field talks to Herb Ross about Julia. In the movie, Sally is Julia's mother. Now the two women are friends. People love *Steel Magnolias*. Julia is Shelby, a sick young woman. She wins an award for her role. She falls in love again, too, with actor Dylan McDermott.

In 1989, Disney starts a new movie, a love story about a beautiful woman, Vivian (Julia Roberts), and a business-man (Richard Gere). *Pretty Woman* makes $450,000,000. People watch the story and fall in love with Vivian. She is beautiful, smart, and fun. Before *Pretty Woman*, Julia Roberts is an interesting young actress. After it, she's a superstar. Every director in Hollywood is calling her.

Julia starts *Flatliners* in October, 1989, and falls in love
with Kiefer Sutherland, an actor in the movie. Julia and
Kiefer have fun. They go to bars. They drive to new places.
Julia buys an expensive car and a big house. They talk
about a big Hollywood wedding for June 14, 1991. On
June 11, Julia stops the wedding. She goes to Ireland with
a new boyfriend, Jason Patric, Kiefer's very good friend.

The year 1991 is difficult for Julia. She makes three movies. *Sleeping with the Enemy* is a big hit, but *Dying Young* and *Hook* are not. She makes *Hook* for director Steven Spielberg. Later he says on TV, "I can't work with Julia Roberts again." Julia can't understand this. Julia stops work for about two years.

Hollywood asks, "Where's our famous superstar?"

Julia is smiling again in 1993. She gets $8,000,000 for the role of Darby Shaw in *The Pelican Brief*. The movie is a big hit and makes $200,000,000. Julia is back! Then, she falls in love again. In New Orleans she meets Lyle Lovett, a tall, quiet, 35-year-old musician.

Julia and Lyle's wedding is about one month later, on June 27, 1993. Julia is beautiful in a white dress and no shoes.

Julia is Mrs. Lyle Lovett for only twenty-one months. She and Lyle are in love, but they are never in the same place. They get a divorce in 1995. Julia is very unhappy.

Julia thinks about movies again, but 1995–6 aren't good years for her. In *Mary Reilly*, Julia has no smile, and she isn't beautiful. *Michael Collins* (with Liam Neeson again) is slow and serious. The movies don't make much money.

People like Julia Roberts in smart love stories. In 1997, she makes *My Best Friend's Wedding*. Many people buy tickets for this movie. It's a big hit and it makes $275,000,000. Then Julia is in New York, in October, 1997, and she meets a new boyfriend, actor Benjamin Bratt. She's with him for four years. Do they talk about a wedding? "Maybe one day," Julia says. But there is no wedding.

From 1997 to 2001, people love Julia in *Conspiracy Theory*, *Stepmom*, *Notting Hill*, *Runaway Bride* (with Richard Gere again), *Erin Brockovitch*, and *The Mexican*. Some good actors get $20,000,000 for a movie. Julia Roberts is the first $20,000,000 actress. She's famous, but she's unhappy about her brother, Eric. Eric and Julia have many old problems, and they don't talk.

"And the winner is Julia Roberts for her role in *Erin Brockovitch*!"

It's March 25, 2001, the night of the Academy Awards.★

"I love the world! I'm very happy!" says Julia.

And tomorrow? Who knows? But today, she looks at her first Oscar and smiles her superstar smile.

★ Academy Awards (Oscars): awards for very good actors.

ACTIVITIES

Before you read

1 What do you know about Julia Roberts and her movies?

2 Answer the questions. Find the words in italics in your dictionary.

   a Where can you see *actors* and *actresses*?

   b How many *brothers* and *sisters* do you have?

   c How much *work* do you do at school?

   d How old are *students* in a *high school*?

   e What comes first, a *divorce* or a *wedding*?

   f Where do you and your *friends* have *fun*?

   g What is the name of a famous *award*, *movie director*, *musician*, and *TV superstar* in your country?

3 Find the words in your dictionary. What are they in your language?

born businessman die fall in love a hit role

serious win world

After you read

4 Why are they important to Julia Roberts?

   a Walter and Betty   **f** Kiefer Sutherland

   b Eric and Lisa   **g** Jason Patric

   c Liam Neeson   **h** Lyle Lovett

   d Sally Field   **i** Benjamin Bratt

   e Richard Gere

5 Why is Julia unhappy in

   a 1972?   **b** 1977?   **c** 1991?   **d** 1995?

6 Why is Julia happy in

   a 1986?   **b** 1989?   **c** 1993?   **d** 2001?